WEATHER AND SEASONS

How this collection works

This collection includes five fascinating non-fiction texts designed to tap into your child's interest in how the weather can be useful and why, as well as the importance of the different seasons we have. These texts are packed full of fascinating information, with the same high-quality artwork and photos you would expect from any non-fiction book – but they are specially written so that your child can read them for themselves. They are carefully levelled and in line with your child's phonics learning at school.

It's very important for your child to have access to non-fiction as well as stories while they are learning to read. This helps them to develop a wider range of reading skills, and prepares them for learning through reading. Most children love finding out about the world as they read – and some children prefer non-fiction to story books, so it's doubly important to make sure that they have opportunities to read both.

How to use this book

Reading should be a shared and enjoyable experience for both you and your child. Pick a time when your child is not distracted by other things, and when they are happy to concentrate for about 10 minutes. Choose one or two of the non-fiction texts for each session, so that they don't get too tired. Read the tips on the next page, as they offer ideas and suggestions for getting the most out of this collection.

Tips for reading non-fiction

STEP 1

Before your child begins reading one of the non-fiction texts, look together at the contents page for that particular text. What does your child think the text will be about? Do they know anything about this subject already? Briefly talk about your child's ideas, and remind them of anything they know about the topic if necessary. Look at the topic words and other notes for each text, and use the 'before reading' suggestions to help introduce the text to your child.

STEP 2

Point out some of the non-fiction features in the text – for example, the contents page, and any photographs. Talk about how the contents page helps you find the different parts of the text, and the photographs help show that this is a book about the real world rather than a story.

STEP 3

Ask your child to read the text aloud. Encourage them to stop and look at the pictures, and talk about what they are reading either during the reading session, or afterwards. Your child will be able to read most of the words in the text, but if they struggle with a word, remind them to say the sounds in the word from left to right and then blend the sounds together to read the whole word, e.g. *d-o-g, dog*. If they have real difficulty, tell them the word and move on.

STEP 4

When your child has finished reading, talk about what they have found out. Which bits of the text did they like most, and why? Encourage your child to do some of the fun activities that follow each text.

CONTENTS

Sun Hat, Sunscreen, Sun!

This text explores how you can be prepared, whatever the weather!

Before reading

Talk about what the weather is like today. What clothes would your child need to wear if they were going outside?

Topic words

These words may be challenging to read but they are important for the topic. Read them together and talk about what they mean.

rain – drops of water that fall from the clouds

wind – movement of the air

snow – small white flakes of frozen rain

Tricky words

These words are common but your child might find them difficult to read:

the, I, for

SUN HAT, SUNSCREEN, SUN!

CONTENTS

Teresa Heapy

I am set for fun in the sun.

8

I am set for a run in the wind.

13

I am set for fun in the snow.

Dressed for the Weather

sun

rain

wind

snow

Talk about it!

What's your favourite type of weather? What clothes do you need to wear for this weather?

Match the weather

Match the weather words to the correct symbols.

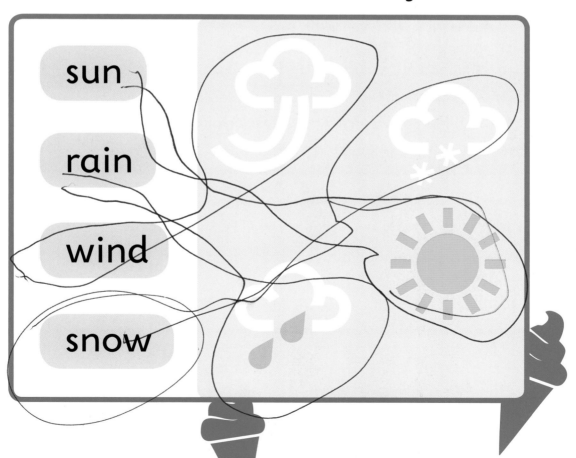

sun

rain

wind

snow

Seasons

This text explores the four different seasons and what happens in each one.

Before reading

Does your child know what season it is at the moment? Talk about the signs you can see outside, that let you know what season it is (trees, birds, flowers, weather).

Topic words

These words may be challenging to read but they are important for the topic. Read them together and talk about what they mean.

spring – the season when things start growing again after winter

summer – the warmest season of the year

autumn – the season when leaves change colour and fall

winter – the coldest season of the year

Tricky words

These words are common but your child might find them difficult to read:

to, there

SEASONS

CONTENTS

Teresa Heapy

Spring

eggs

frog

There is a lot to spot in spring.

1

2

frog eggs

4

3

Summer

nest

There is a lot to spot in summer.

23

Autumn

Lots to peck!

There is a lot to spot in autumn.

Winter

frost

twigs

There is a lot to spot in winter.

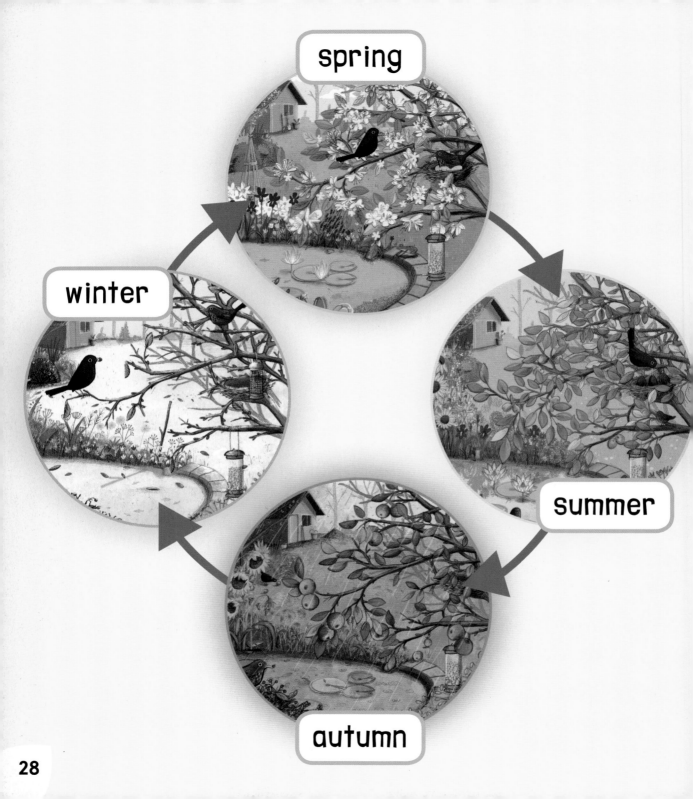

spring

summer

autumn

winter

28

Talk about it!

Which is your favourite season? Why?

Season match!

Match the pictures to the correct season.

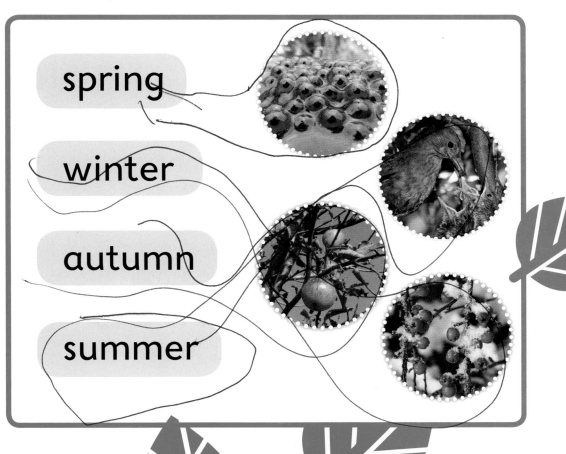

spring

winter

autumn

summer

Day and Night

This text explores what we do at different times of the day.

Before reading

Talk about what your child does at different times of the day. Can they think of some things they do at the same time every day?

Topic words

These words may be challenging to read but they are important for the topic. Read them together and talk about what they mean.

morning – the first part of the day, before lunchtime

afternoon – the second part of the day, after lunchtime

evening – the third part of the day, when the sun goes down

night-time – the end of the day, when it is dark

Tricky words

These words are common but your child might find them difficult to read:

the, you

DAY AND NIGHT

CONTENTS

Teresa Heapy

Kim

It is the morning.
Can you spot Kim?

It is the afternoon.
Can you spot Kim?

35

It is the evening.
Can you spot Kim?

36

37

It is night-time.
Can you spot Kim?

39

Talk about it!

What is your favourite time of day? Why?

Spot it!

Look back through the text. Can you spot these people?

In the Wind

This text explores how the wind can make things move in different ways.

Before reading

Talk about what it is like being outdoors on a windy day. What kinds of things move in the wind?

Topic words

These words may be challenging to read but they are important for the topic. Read them together and talk about what they mean.

makes – creates, causes to happen

things – objects

wind – movement of the air

along – going in a certain direction

Tricky words

These words are common but your child might find them difficult to read:

the, go, of

IN THE WIND

CONTENTS

Catherine Baker

Go!

The wind makes lots of things go!

Along

The wind makes things go along.

The man can go along in the wind!

along

Spin

The wind makes things spin.

spin

The mill
can spin
in the wind.

Up

Things can go up in the wind.

up

The wind can lift things up, up, up!

In the Wind

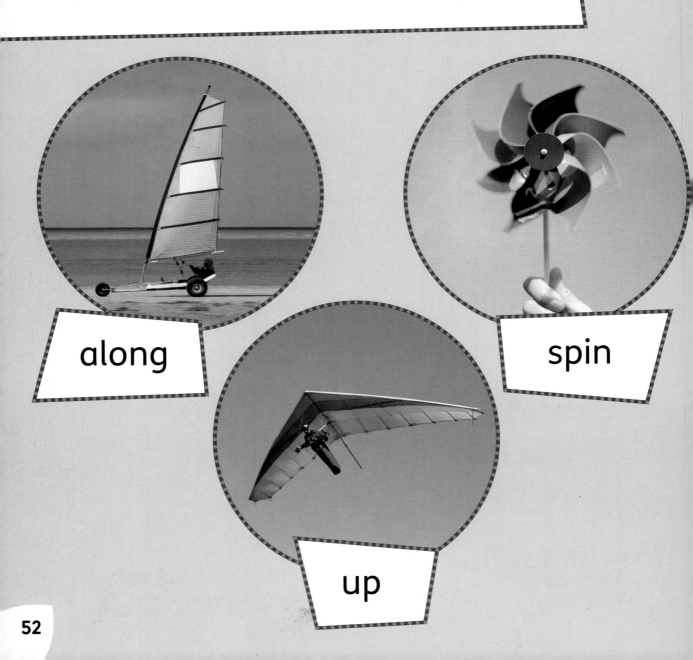

along

spin

up

Talk about it!

What would you like to do on a windy day? Why?

Maze

Can you help the boat win the race?

Rain!

This text explores why rain is surprisingly good!

Before reading

Does your child like going out in the rain? What is good about it?
What is not so good?

Topic words

These words may be challenging to read but they are important
for the topic. Read them together and talk about what they mean.

water – the clear liquid from taps, rivers and the sea

rain – water that falls from the clouds

rivers – large streams of water that flow along the ground

clean – not dirty

lakes – flat, still areas of water

Tricky words

These words are common but your child might find them difficult
to read:

I, go, into, the, of

RAIN!

CONTENTS

Becca Heddle

Rain is lots of drops of water.

Plants get water from the rain.

61

Rain runs into rivers. It fills the rivers up.

It is fun on the lakes.

And I can get clean in the water.

Rain Is Not Bad!

Talk about it!

What do you like to do in the rain? Why?

Choose

What is rain good for? Tick the boxes.

ACTIVITIES

Match the seasons

Match the seasons to the things you might see.

spring   summer   autumn   winter

Weather word search

Find the weather words!

r	a	s	h	o	t	k
a	u	u	s	n	e	e
i	a	i	u	c	c	s
n	f	f	n	i	c	n
c	d	l	e	r	o	o
t	h	o	r	s	l	w
w	i	n	d	o	d	g

wind   rain   cold

snow   sun   hot

74

Spot the difference!

Can you spot three differences between these pictures?

Rain maze

Help the rain drop go all the way down the river to the sea.